XANDER'S STORY

D1384861

by Alejandro & Christopher Garcia-Halenar

Special thanks to:

-John and Cliff and the entire team at Rosie's. Your restaurant will always be a special place for us – not just because this is where we met, but because of how much you give back to the community – A.G-H. & C.G-H.

-Jennifer Little and her extremely talented staff at Little's Photography. Your exceptional work was the inspiration for the front and back cover of Xander's Story. You guys are genius – A.G-H. & C.G-H.

Illustrations by: Richa Kinra Shekhar Arts

We never knew someone so small
could make our lives so big...
We love you the MOSTEST!

One day in a magical place called "Rosie's" Daddy and Papa met and they fell in love they enjoyed every minute of their time together

they travelled
the world

they enjoyed the outdoors

they celebrated life with
friends and family

but they wanted more –
They wanted a **FAMILY**

Daddy and Papa began their journey to start a FAMILY

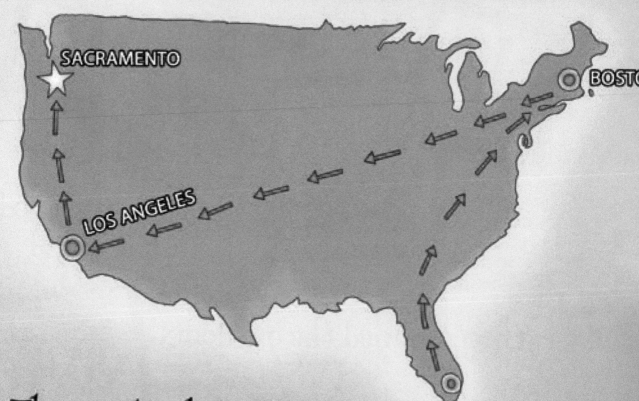

SACRAMENTO

BOSTO

LOS ANGELES

FORT LAUDERDALE

They realized starting a FAMILY was really, really hard

They needed
3 things...

The **1**st thing Daddy and Papa needed was the **PERFECT EGG**

All babies start as an egg
and they grow and grow
until they become a little baby

Daddy and Papa began their search for the

PERFECT EGG

...they looked in the cupboard

...they looked in a tree

FINALLY, they found a beautiful girl with
LOTS OF EGGS

She was kind and generous
and gave Daddy and Papa the

THE PERFECT EGG

The **2ⁿᵈ** thing Daddy and Papa needed was the PERFECT PLACE to keep the EGG

They needed a place that was
SAFE and **WARM**
so the little EGG could grow

They looked in the oven...

They looked
under the covers...

FINALLY, they found a smart and beautiful woman named Auntie Stacie who had the **PERFECT PLACE**

Auntie Stacie was very, very
★ SPECIAL ★

She helped Daddy and Papa put the
PERFECT EGG in the PERFECT PLACE

The PERFECT EGG
LVED
being in
Auntie Stacie's belly

The EGG grew
until it was
the size of an
orange

The EGG grew
until it was
the size of a
bean

Finally after the EGG grew and grew for 9 whole months

The EGG grew until it was the size of a football

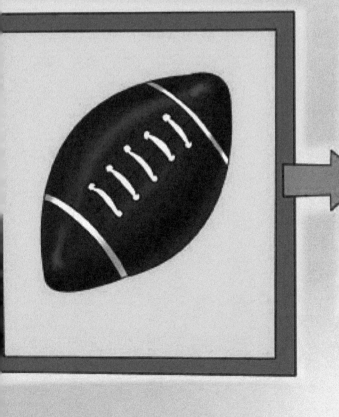

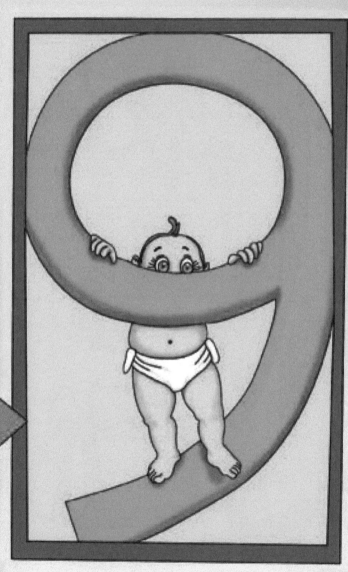

The EGG was ready to meet Daddy and Papa

Auntie Stacie whispered to the EGG,
"It's time to be born little egg"

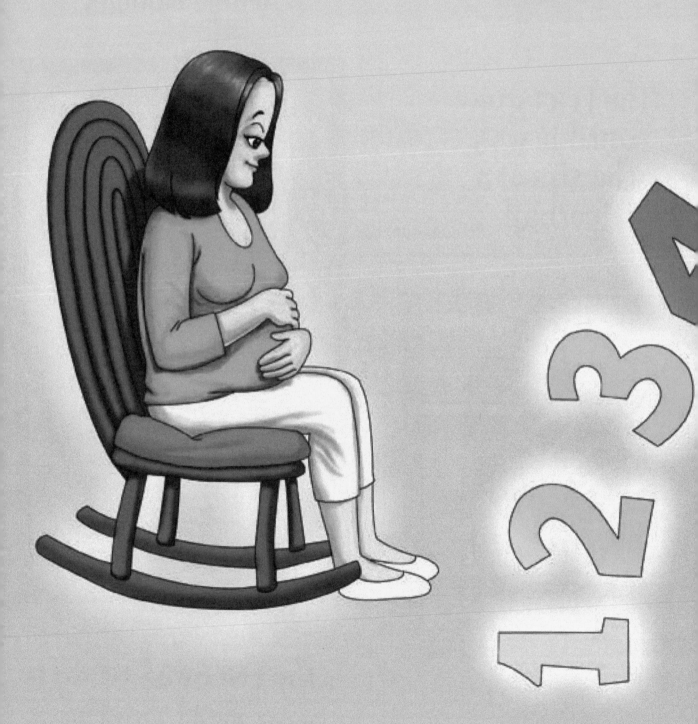

5 6 7 8 9 MONTHS

But the EGG was no longer an EGG

After 9 months of Auntie Stacie taking care of and loving the EGG The little EGG grew into a beautiful little BABY

The **3rd** and final thing Daddy and Papa needed to complete their family was L♥VE

...we didn't need to look in the cupboard

...we didn't need to look under the cover

...we didn't need to look high or low

HIGH
LOW

WE HAD LOVE ALL ALONG

We loved you when you were the PERFECT EGG

We loved you when you were growing in the PERFECT PLACE

And we loved you on that special night you were born

LOVE is what inspired our SPECIAL FAMILY

And our LOVE grows more and more each day!

About Xander's Family:

Xander, his little brother Max, and his two Dads, Alex and Chri[s] Garcia-Halenar, live in South Florida. Both Alex and Chris always wanted a family and began their surrogacy journey soo[n] after falling in love. Believing that every child's story is unique and should be celebrated, they wrote this book so their son will always know how special he is.

We LOVE you XANDER

TO THE
MOON
AND BACK!

Love,
Daddy and Papa

Lightning Source UK Ltd.
Milton Keynes UK
UKHW050822220120
357223UK00007B/5